SAVING the LIBERTY BELL

For Jordan, Nathan, and Chloe
—M. M.

To Kevin,
April 9, 2001, and the rest is history
—M. G. C.

Atheneum Books for Young Readers • An imprint of Simon & Schuster Children's Publishing Division • 1230 Avenue of the Americas, New York, New York 10020 • Text copyright © 2005 by Megan McDonald • Illustrations copyright © 2005 by Marsha Gray Carrington • All rights reserved, including the right of reproduction in whole or in part in any form. • Book design by Sonia Chaghatzbanian • The text of this book is set in Carré Noir Medium. • The illustrations are rendered in acrylic paint. • Manufactured in China • 10 9 8 7 6 5 4 • Library of Congress Cataloging-in-Publication Data • McDonald, Megan. • Saving the Liberty Bell / Megan McDonald ; illustrated by Marsha Gray Carrington. • p. cm. • "A Richard Jackson Book." • ISBN 0-689-85167-7 • 1. Mickley, Johnny—Juvenile literature. 2. Liberty Bell—Juvenile literature. 3. Philadelphia (Pa.)—History—Revolution, 1775-1783—Juvenile literature. I. Carrington, Marsha Gray, ill. II. Title. • F158.8.I3 M38 2005 • 974.8'11—dc22 • 2004012703

SAVING the Liberty BELL

STORY BY
MEGAN McDONALD

ILLUSTRATIONS BY
MARSHA GRAY CARRINGTON

A RICHARD JACKSON BOOK
Atheneum Books for Young Readers
New York   London   Toronto   Sydney

John Jacob limped up to the front door. It was good to be home, home to the smell of Mama's wild-cherry pie baking. Home to the arms of his brothers and sisters around his waist.

"John-John! Where have you been?" asked Magdalena.

"Mama will not tell us!" said Christian.

"Can you keep a secret?" John Jacob whispered. "I have been . . . to Philadelphia!"

'Twas black as black night when Papa and I loaded up the wagon, and first blue light by the time we were on our way. After days of so much bumping on the road, I felt my bones were being rearranged. I was sure and certain I would not be the same person seeing Philadelphia as when I left home.

Brong! Brong! Bronnggg! rang the Great Bell atop the State House. The sound of that bell hung like a storm cloud over the city, calling out a warning: "Redcoats! The Redcoats are coming!" Word spread around like wildfire!

Bling! Blang! Blong! Church bells rang and clanged, answering back, "Make haste! Hide all valuables! Away with all supplies! Save them from the English!"

See, General Howe and his troops were on the march. And sure as my name's John Jacob Mickley, they'd be looting and stealing any metal they could get their British hands on. Copper! Lead! Brass! House gutters! Even the door knockers! They aimed to melt it all down for musket shot. Or worse . . . cannons!

And what do you think would make them the biggest prize of all? The Great Bell!

Amid the flurry, Papa and I unloaded our farm goods. We were in the stables, feeding and watering Kit and June, when a man by the name of Colonel Benjamin Flower came up to us. He liked the looks of our horses and asked about our wagon.

Next thing I knew, we—I mean, Papa and me, . . . I mean, our very own Mickley wagon—had been chosen to help the Revolution.

Shh! You musn't say a word, now. Our mission was to hide something big, something important and meaningful, something as great as gold, in our wagon. To spirit it away in the middle of the night and see it to safety, back in our own Northampton Towne.

And what do you think it was?

Heigh-ho! 'Twas the Great Bell!

I, your own humble brother, was to ride in the very same wagon. Papa said, "We must wait now, till the darkest hour. Midnight. Why, any passing face could be that of a spy for the British."

I do believe all of Philadelphia held its breath that night. Not a dog's bark. Not a baby's cry. The Bell waited for us in silence, a voice with no tongue.

"Papa!" I whispered. "That bell stands half as tall as a man."

"And weighs more than two thousand pounds," said Papa.

As soon as the Bell was loaded onto the wagon, I rubbed my fingers across its shoulder, trying to read the words of freedom written there. Papa told me they said, "Proclaim LIBERTY throughout all the Land unto all the Inhabitants thereof." I took those words straight to heart and held them there for the entire journey.

Now, if you're wondering how we hid such a thing as a bell that size, I'll tell you. We heaped mounds of stable straw atop the Bell to cover it up. And potato sacks and such, not to mention, of all things, a lady's hoop skirt! That stable straw did stink to high heaven, so who would have thought of hiding a bell under there?

We left town, a parade without a marching beat. Our wagon gave out squeaky creaks at every turn and groaned like a cow birthing a calf until I thought for sure and certain those Redcoats would be upon us.

"Papa, what will happen if they catch us?" I whispered.

"Here, take the reins," Papa said. "Fix your mind on something besides Redcoats."

As I drove the wagon north to Bethlehem, Papa told me not to worry. He said the Redcoats would be fooled into believing the Bell, along with ten or more church bells, was moving east, to be sunk into the Delaware River!

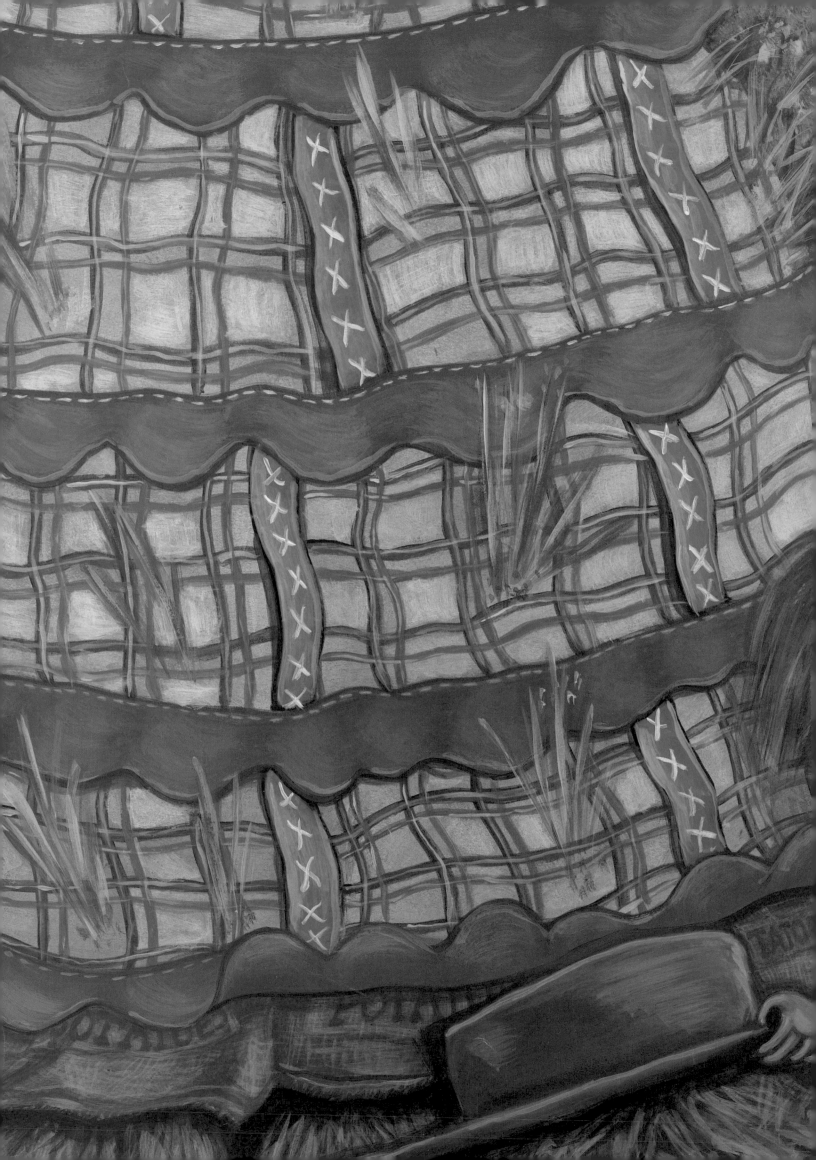

By the third night out, I'd hardly caught a wink of sleep. But I must have drifted off, because I awoke to the sound of a thousand hoofbeats. Redcoats!

Not in all my eleven years has my heart thumped so, louder than the distant drums. Every crack of cannon fire turned my nerves to popping corn. I leaned against the Bell and closed my eyes, willing myself steady.

We soon hid our wagon in a small stand of trees along the Bethlehem Road. It was near morning light. I prayed silently in my head that the shadows would hide us. That Kit and June would not start whinnying. That my rattling teeth would not give us away.

Leaves crunched. Twigs snapped. Footsteps.

"Who goes there?" called a soldier.

I peered around a tree trunk.

"Boy! You there! Show yourself! Tell me, in the name of General Washington, what business you have here!"

General Washington! I could not believe my ears. 'Twas not a Redcoat I saw, but a soldier of Washington's own Continental Army. A patriot!

I could see soldiers, horses, and wagons snaking from the horizon—seven hundred wagons and near three thousand horses. What a sight! Washington's army, right here in Lehigh Valley, on their way to winter quarters. That Bell couldn't have been safer. The army escorted us right into Bethlehem, where the orange-tipped trees of our own valley waved us a welcome.

But four miles from home: *Crrr-aaack!*

Just when I thought the Bell was safe, I heard an ear-splitting sound. "Papa!" I shouted. There, in the middle of a square full of onlookers, came a great splintering of wood like lightning striking a tree, then *crash!*

"The Bell!" I cried as our wagon broke, and I tumbled to the ground right along with it. My foot turned near to the ankle and swelled like a puffball. I am sorry to have to tell you that I did yawl like a dying cat, sprawled there in the mud while the wheelwright made haste to fix the front wagon wheel.

"Hurry!" Papa urged. "Anyone in that curious crowd might prove to be a spy for General Howe!"

There was no hiding our prize now, so the farmers hoisted the Bell onto a stout wagon nearby, that of Mr. Frederick Leaser. My spirit splintered at the thought of not seeing the Great Bell to safety in Northampton Towne. That's when the kind Mr. Leaser offered, "Ride along with me. You've come this far with the Bell and cannot abandon it now."

After the sixth night had fallen since we left Philadelphia, our wagons rattled toward home. My heart leaped high as a summer frog when I could make out the church steeple sticking up through the trees. Who should we find waiting for us on Hamilton Street but a red-faced Reverend Blumer, who'd stripped off his jacket, rolled up his sleeves, and plied loose the planks, tearing up the floor of the Zion Reformed Church.

"Shh! Listen close, my brothers and sisters, for I am passing this secret on to you. You must do your part by keeping your lips sealed as tight as hoops on a barrel. We did spirit away and hide the Great Bell of Philadelphia under those dusty floorboards! Cross my heart, that's the truth.

"Think of it there, lifting up your feet this Sabbath as you sing your hymns to heaven. But promise me you will keep my secret. And Papa's. And all the good folks of Northampton Towne. Swear in the name of George Washington that you will never, not ever, tell a soul.

"Your voices, like that bell, must be silent. Waiting. Hoping. Hoping in your hearts for freedom to ring again."

Historical Note

The Great Bell rang for freedom on July 8, 1776, to mark the first public reading of the Declaration of Independence. Though a topic of much debate, the commonly accepted date for the cracking of the Bell (as we know it today) is July 8, 1835. The State House Bell did not come to be called the Liberty Bell until the 1840s, when the American Anti-slavery Society adopted it as a symbol of freedom. Lesser known is its role in the American Revolution, when the Bell was secreted away from the State House (now Independence Hall) in Philadelphia and hidden beneath the floorboards of present-day Allentown's Zion Reformed Church.

Controversy exists over who actually hauled the Bell, but history has settled on John Jacob Mickley's wagon as carrying it as far as Bethlehem, where it broke down and was transferred to the wagon of Frederick Leaser. John Jacob Mickley had ten children: Catherine, John Jacob, Christian, Peter, Henry, Joseph, Daniel, Sarah, Anna, and Magdalena. His oldest son, John Jacob, then eleven years old, rode in the wagon with the Bell and was sometimes allowed to take the reins. Church bells from St. Peter's and Christ Church were also removed from the city. Perhaps eleven or twelve bells in all were sent into hiding. Rumors soon tricked the British into thinking the bells had been sunk into the Delaware River.

Dirt, hay, straw, and manure were most likely used to conceal the Bell. Potato sacks and a lady's hoop skirt are part of the lore that has been passed down along with the story. The wagons did meet up with Washington's army, who offered them protection. Nearly a year later, on June 18, 1778, the British General Howe and his army evacuated Philadelphia and made possible the return of the bells to that city. No longer silent, the Great Bell became a voice for the people, proclaiming liberty throughout the land. Today, and for all time, the Liberty Bell stands as a symbol of independence and revolutionary spirit.